Ginger snaps

Fun Thoughts on Life

COMPILED BY

Dian Ritter

ILLUSTRATED BY

Sally Goodling

Published by The C. R. Gibson Company
Norwalk, Connecticut

The material contained in this book was collected over a period of years from a variety of sources. Many of the original authors are unknown and some of the materials have been attributed to more than one author. I have found that many of the words of wisdom are paraphrased from the wisdom of Solomon found in *Proverbs*. Since it is impossible to list each author, I would like this book to be an acknowledgment of appreciation to the authors for their words of wit and wisdom.

Dian Ritter

Ginger Snaps

FUN THOUGHTS ON LIFE

CONTENTS

Opportunities • Goals • Success

Opportunity is sometimes hard to recognize
if you are only looking for a lucky break.

Opportunity knocks, but you have to open the door.

The label on the door to opportunity reads PUSH.

The trouble with opportunity is that it always looks better
going than coming.

Opportunity is like an egg—once it is dropped,
its composure disintegrates.

Jumping at several small opportunities
may get us there more quickly
than waiting for one big one to come along.

The right man is the one who seized the moment.

Weak men wait for opportunities; strong men make them.

Do you see difficulties in every opportunity,
or opportunity in every difficulty?

To accomplish great things, we must not only act,
but also dream; not only plan, but also believe.

No great man ever complains of the lack of opportunity.

Opportunities take *now* for an answer.

If you're living up to your ideals, they're not high enough.

The best place to start to get any place
is where you happen to be.

The road of life may be hard at times, but to reach your goals
you must keep to the right.

The man without a purpose is like a ship without a
rudder—a waif, a nothing, a non-man.

We all live under the same sky,
but we don't all have the same horizon.

Most people don't recognize opportunity when it comes along
because it is usually disguised as hard work.

The most important part of getting what you want
is knowing what you want.

The largest room in the world is the room for improvement.

Beaten paths are for beaten men.

When you kill a little time,
you may be murdering opportunity.

The longer you wait for your golden opportunity,
the brassier it becomes.

The trouble with not having a goal is that you can spend your
life running up and down the field and never scoring.

You cannot find happiness
until your goal is clear and in view.

If you want to get ahead, make sure you use the one you have.

The trouble with success is that the formula is the same as the
one for a nervous breakdown.

An opportunist is one who goes ahead and does what you had
always been planning to do.

There's no such thing as a ladder of success—
it's a greased pole.

To whom much is given, much therefore is expected.

It's doing your job the best you can,
And being just to your fellow man.
It's figuring how, and learning why
And looking forward and thinking high:
And dreaming little and doing much:
It's keeping always in closest touch
With what is finest in word and deed:
It's being clean, and it's playing fair:
It's laughing lightly at Dame Despair;
It's sharing sorrow, and work, and mirth,
And making better this good old earth:
It's serving and striving through strain
    and stress
It's doing your noblest—that's success.

In everything you do, put God first, and He will direct you and crown your efforts with success.

If at first you don't succeed, try looking in the wastebasket for the directions.

Be nice to others on your way up and maybe they'll be nice to you on your way down.

All adverse and depressing influences can be overcome, not by fighting, but by rising above them.

It will do no good to get on the right track
if you are headed in the wrong direction.

There isn't much thrill in success
unless one has first been close to failure.

Great trials seem to be necessary preparation
for great duties.

There are no hopeless situations; there are only men who have grown hopeless about them.

To do for the world more than the world does for you—that is success.

The man who tries to chase two rabbits at the same time seldom catches either.

He who gains a victory over other men is strong; but he who gains a victory over himself is all powerful.

You can't expect to become well-heeled
unless you're on your toes.

Some few may strike it rich, but we'd
Accept it on authority
That if at first you don't succeed,
You're with the vast majority.

Great ideas need landing gears as well as wings.

Those who try most will fail most.

Bloom where you are planted.

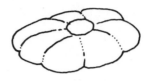

If you are not afraid to face the music, you may someday lead the band.

A friend is always delighted at your success, provided it doesn't exceed his own.

A genius is a man who takes the lemons that Fate hands him and starts a lemonade stand with them.

A person doesn't get very far in this world if he has to spend a lot of time covering up his tracks.

Few people learn from success, but there is often much to learn from failure.

Never give up on a man until he has failed at something that he likes.

Most successful men are married; but so are most failures.

What on earth would a man do with himself if something did not stand in his way?

Perhaps you cannot be a star, but you need not be a cloud!

Stickability is 95 per cent of ability.

Success is not always final. If you build a better mousetrap, nature will breed a smarter mouse.

Behind every successful man stands a woman who couldn't be more surprised.

There's nothing wrong with being a self-made man if you don't consider the job finished too soon.

Failure is delay, but not defeat.

Don't expect to make others as you wish them to be when you can't make yourself as you wish to be.

Think doubt and fail
Think victory and succeed.

The highest reward for man's toil is not what he gets for it, but what he becomes by it.

The only time you mustn't fail is the last time you try.

Patience is power; with time and patience the mulberry leaf becomes silk.

Success is speaking words of praise
In cheering other people's ways
In doing just the best you can
With every task and every plan
It's silence when your speech would hurt
Politeness when your neighbor's curt
It's deafness when the scandal flows
And sympathy with others' woes
It's loyalty when duty calls
It's courage when disaster falls
It's found in laughter and in song
It's in the silent time of prayer
In happiness and in despair
In all of life and nothing less
We find the thing we call success.

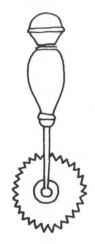

The reward of a thing well done is to have done it.

Starting out to make money is the greatest mistake in life. Do what you feel you have a flair for doing, and if you are good enough at it, the money will come.

No man ever yet became great by imitation.

The road to success always has detours.

Success tip: Start at the bottom and wake up.

I will . . . because I can.

What is easy is seldom excellent.

Only he who attempts the ridiculous can achieve the impossible.

Anyone who begins the day's work with reluctance and ends it with joy will never be a howling success at anything.

Your ship likely won't come in till you send it out.

A leader has two important characteristics: First, he is going somewhere; second, he is able to persuade others to go with him.

Success is seldom an accident or an incident;
it is the result.

Integrity is the first step to true greatness.

If you fail to prepare, prepare to fail.

Success is not a harbor, but a voyage with its own perils to the spirit.

It is not a question of who's going to throw the first stone; it's a question of who's going to start building with it.

We can't all be heroes because someone has to sit on the curb and clap as they go by.

Every man is a self-made man,
but only successful men admit it.

It is impossible to gain a toehold on success
by acting like a heel.

Mistakes are simply invitations to try again.

Live for Today
Dream for Tomorrow
Learn from Yesterday.

Whatever it is you want, you reach a long way toward it if you will combine your heart, your backbone, your faith, and your common sense, and then stretch.

All of us would be famous if it didn't take any time, work, or thought.

We are what we repeatedly do.
Excellence, then, is not an act but a habit.

All men want to succeed; some want to succeed so badly that they're willing to work for it.

Success does not consist in never making mistakes, but in never making the same mistake the second time.

Failure to hit the bull's eye
is never the fault of the target.

The big things that come our way are seldom the result of long-thought-out and careful planning, but rather they are the fruit of seeds planted in the daily routine of work.

When you've set your mind to do it,
When your judgment says you're right,
When your conscience gives it sanction,
Then pitch in with all your might.

Don't let anything prevent you,
Though the odds seem big and strong.
Every obstacle will vanish
As the swift days roll along—
If you set your jaws and say,
"Well, I'll do it anyway."

If you want to follow in your father's footsteps,
don't wear loafers.

Few people ever carve their way to success
with cutting remarks.

The harder you work, the luckier you get.

When you can't find your station in life,
somebody will tell you where to get off.

By three things you will be known and remembered—
truthfulness, faithfulness, and friendliness.

A truly successful person is willing
to earn more than he receives.

Accomplishment is ability stripped of its doubts.

Success is effort draped in day-to-day self-improvement.

Success is biting off more than you can chew—then chewing it.

Everyone is interested in improving—his wife,
his children, his company, and his country.

Greatness is never something conferred;
it is something achieved.

Hitting the ceiling is a poor way to rise in the world.

The best way out is always through.

The victory of success is half won
when one gains the habit of work.

The surface swimmer makes the splash,
but the deep diver brings up the pearls.

If at first you succeed,
try hard to hide your astonishment.

Man cannot discover new oceans unless he has the courage to
lose sight of the shore.

God never puts any man in a space too small to grow in.

Your attitude determines your altitude.

You cannot antagonize and influence at the same time.

The door to the room of success
swings on the hinges of opposition.

Anyone who isn't pulling his weight is pushing his luck.

If at first you succeed, try something harder.

Work Habits • Business • Jobs

The worker whose heart is in his pay envelope is seldom likely to become the filler of pay envelopes for others.

There aren't enough crutches in the world
for all the lame excuses.

Nothing is particularly hard
if you divide it into small jobs.

Never confuse motion with action.

The best way to appreciate your job
is to imagine yourself without it.

The best way to break a habit is to drop it.

Work done with little effort may yield little fruit.

Don't wish for more than you are willing to work for.

Habits are first cobwebs, then cables.

This world would be wonderful if we all did as well as we expect to do tomorrow.

The unfortunate thing about this world is that good habits are so much easier to get out of than bad ones.

Cultivate good habits—the bad ones all grow wild.

People who dig are seldom in the hole.

Often it is easier to do a good job
than to explain why you didn't.

Grandpa used a tranquilizer, too; he called it work.

No one can be completely relaxed. Like a windup clock, a person can't tick without some tension.

Have a happy tomorrow—do today's work today.

Good judgement comes from experience,
and experience often comes from bad judgement.

Your day goes the way the corners of your mouth turn.

Where all think alike, no one thinks very much.

Time isn't your enemy unless you try to kill it.

The worst boss anyone can have is a bad habit.

By the work one knows the workman.

There is no traffic jam on the "extra mile."

As long as the day lasts, let's give it all we have.

The chap who says, "What's the use?"
is never the engine, always the caboose.

The difference between a job and a career
is the difference between 40 and 60 hours a week.

A man doesn't live by bread alone.
He needs buttering up once in a while.

He who ceases to be better, ceases to be good.

The hardest thing to get is going.

If there is no wind, row.

If you're going around in circles,
maybe it's because you're cutting too many corners.

Only those who have the patience to do simple things
perfectly ever acquire the skill to do difficult things easily.

Anyone can do any amount of work, provided it isn't the work
he is supposed to be doing.

Nothing is really work unless you would rather be doing
something else.

When your work speaks for itself, don't interrupt.

Early to bed and early to rise enables you to save enough to do
otherwise.

Do the right thing because it is the right thing to do.

It is better to burn the candle at both ends, and in the middle,
too, than to put it away in the closet and let the mice eat it.

Never cut what you can untie.

If you stop every time a dog barks,
you will never get there.

If it is difficult, we do it immediately;
if it is impossible, it may take a little longer.

If the power to do hard work is not a talent,
it is the best possible substitute for it.

Some people are so busy learning the tricks of the trade that
they never learn the trade.

The symptoms of laziness and fatigue
are practically identical.

Our first energy crisis was known as Monday morning.

Don't put off until tomorrow
what you can do at overtime rates today.

The only thing worse than getting up early to go to work is
getting up early with no work to go to.

The only people who succumb to hard work are those who kill
themselves dodging it.

The man who tries to dodge his responsibilities usually finds
the detour rougher than the road.

People work harder and smarter if they find their work
satisfying and know that it is appreciated.

One of the tests of leadership is the ability to recognize a
problem before it becomes an emergency.

Perhaps we're worrying too much about automation taking our
jobs. Whenever a traffic jam gets really bad, they turn off the
traffic lights and bring in a policeman.

The man, who complained that being
Just a cog in the wheel was hard,
Has now progressed to where he is
Ten holes in a computer card.

You are not dressed for work until you wear a smile.

It's often difficult to decide whether
we're tired—or just lazy.

Almost everyone wants to be better, but not right now.

If you growl all day,
you can expect to be dog-tired at night.

A horse can't pull while kickin'—
This fact I'll only mention.
But a horse can't kick while pullin'
Is really my contention.

Let's be like a good old horse
And live a life that's fittin'.
Just pull a good honest load
And there'll be no time for kickin'.

Too many meetings are held each month for no better reason
than that it has been a month since the last one.

Glamour is when the value of the package exceeds that of the
contents.

Both optimists and pessimists contribute to our society. The
optimist invents the airplane and the pessimist the parachute.

Praise is a device for making a man deserve it.

The reason the Ten Commandments are short and sweet is that
they were handed down direct, not through several
committees.

There are two kinds of fools. One says, "This is old; therefore, it
is good." The other says, "This is new; therefore, it is better."

Shorthand is a device used by secretaries to make you wonder
what you really said.

Anything in life worth having is worth working for.

Another thing this country needs—a shopping cart with four wheels that all go in the same direction.

An efficiency expert is one who can tell you how to run your business, but isn't smart enough to start one of his own.

If the current TV shows keep on the way they are going, the public will soon be demanding longer commercials.

A company is known by the men it keeps.

A coffee break is when the second cup is free.

The beauty of the old-fashioned blacksmith was that when you brought him your horse to be shod, he didn't think of 40 other things that ought to be done.

Put a grain of boldness in everything you do.

Ah, the insight of hindsight!

A pat on the back, though a few vertebrae removed from a kick in the pants, is miles ahead in results.

Moderation in temper is always a virtue,
but moderation in principle is always a vice.

You can't expect a person to see eye to eye with you when you are looking down on him.

Indifference is something that others
pay back to you with interest.

Tact is the ability to build a fire under people without making their blood boil.

The heaviest load to carry is a bundle of grudges.

Doing beats stewing.

The final test of a gentleman: his respect for those who can be of no possible service to him.

The workers are the saviors of society,
the redeemers of the race.

It isn't our position, but our disposition toward our position, that counts.

To err is human; but, to get things really fouled up, it takes a computer.

Good nature is the oil that makes the day's work go without squeaking.

No job has a future—the future is with the person who holds the job.

About the only business that makes money without publicity is the mint.

One reason computers can do more work than people is that they don't have to stop to answer the phone.

The best way to slow up progress is to form a committee to do something about it.

Be nice to co-workers—
Don't be rude, surly, cross
For you never know when
One may end up your boss.

Meticulous is when someone points out a spelling error in a memo. Nit-picking is when you wrote the memo.

The problem with competition is that it brings out the best in products, but the worst in men.

The nearest to perfection most people ever come is when filling out an employment application.

You may look down on your fellow men
That fact is very true—
But that doesn't necessarily mean
They're looking up to you.

The main trouble with going through channels
is that we so often get stuck in a rut.

When some people quit a job,
they leave no vacancy behind them to fill.

For every action there is an equal but opposite
reaction—especially on Mondays.

Don't answer letters—answer people.

A new idea is delicate. It can be killed by a sneer or a yawn; it
can be stabbed to death by a quip and worried to death by a
frown.

The mark of a true executive is usually illegible.

Making up your mind is like making a bed;
it usually helps to have someone on the other side.

The typical successful American businessman was born in the
country, where he worked hard so that he could live in the city,
where he worked hard so that he could live in the country.

Efficiency: making each member of the office staff toe the line.
Regimentation: when it's your toe.

You can always tell who the boss is; he's the one who watches
the clock during coffee breaks.

Business is something, which,
if you don't have any, you go out of.

A business genius is a man who knows the difference between
being let in on a deal and taken in by one.

A Time for Management

Money • Taxes • Government

It's a fast age. The impossibility of yesterday has become the luxury of today and the necessity of tomorrow.

The worst thing about history is that every time it repeats itself, the price goes up.

There is one thing for a man to do who is married to a woman who enjoys spending money and that is to enjoy earning it.

Gambling is a way of getting nothing for something.

Dollars and sense do not always travel together.

Travel broadens the mind, flattens the finances, and lengthens the communication.

Debt is a trap which a man sets and baits himself— and catches himself.

Pretending to be rich keeps many people poor.

More than one pessimist got that way
by financing an optimist.

There, little luxury, don't you cry—
you'll be a necessity by and by.

Love makes the world go around, but cash pays the bills.

Some people have to "moonlight" just to see daylight.

My tastes are simple; I like to have the best.

A little yearning can be a dangerous thing.

The average American worker earns almost twice as much as an Englishman, three times as much as a Russian, and about half of what he thinks he should be earning.

Yesterday's nest egg will hardly buy today's birdhouse.

Good hard cash makes a nice soft place on which to fall.

We would be glad to pay as we go
if we could catch up paying for where we have been.

Many Americans work 50 weeks out of the year to equip their home with comforts and convenience; then spend their vacation in a cabin or tent, with none.

No matter how low the dollar may fall, it will never fall as low as some people will stoop to get it.

Appearances can be deceiving; a ten-dollar bill looks the same as it did ten years ago.

It is possible to give away and become richer. It is also possible to hold on too tightly and lose everything.

A budget is a family's attempt to live below its yearnings.

There is no dignity quite so impressive, and no independence quite so important, as living within your means.

People can stand their own property
better than another's property.

Nothing makes time go faster than buying on it.

It's a big problem to reconcile one's net income
with one's gross habits.

If the average man saves for the next 20 years at the same rate he has been saving for the past 6 months, he'll be able to retire at the age of 60 owing $100,000.

I've tried to put up with this inflation,
But I'm going to lose my endurance
If I have to sell my car
To pay for my auto insurance.

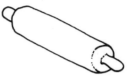

People who think nothing of borrowing money,
think even less of paying it back.

The richest man is the one who finds
pleasures in everyday duties.

You can't take it with you, but that's about the only place you can go without it.

The trouble with a good many cars today is that the engine won't start and the payments won't stop.

People today seem to be able to afford all the luxuries, but they complain bitterly about the cost of necessities.

It's a funny thing about those foreign cars. Most of the people who can afford them can't fit into them.

To feel rich, count the things
that you have that money can't buy.

Most people are too busy earning a living to make any money.

Failure to pay as you go
is what makes the return trip so rough.

The only place where ends meet now is on the football field.

The credit card's a
Wondrous thing
But really has to
Take one knock:
It insulates from
Instant charge—
But wholly fails on
Future shock.

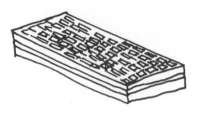

Money is a good servant, but a poor master.

Although a dollar is only six inches long, it is used to measure many things.

It takes a heap of payments to make a house a home.

A dollar may not do as much for us as it used to, but then we don't do as much for a dollar, either.

You should never go into debt
unless you can see your way out.

The secret of financial success is to spend what you have left after saving, instead of saving what you have left after spending.

Being content with your lot
is a lot simpler when you have a lot.

A lot of people go in debt just to keep up
with those who already are.

He is always a slave who cannot live on little.

It's strange that people call money "dough"—
dough sticks to your fingers.

The evil man gets rich for the moment, but the good man's
rewards last forever.

Many folks talk economy,
but few have the will to practice it.

One of the fastest ways to go broke is by auto.

Inflation is a method of cutting a dollar bill in half without
damaging the paper.

Maybe it's called cold cash because few people keep it long
enough to warm it.

One remarkable thing about the dollar is that when it floats, it
sinks.

An acquaintance is a person we know well enough to borrow
from, but not well enough to lend to.

A lot of people just can't stand prosperity—but then,
most people don't have to.

The thoughts of people are more valuable than money. When
two people exchange dollar bills, then each one still has only
one dollar. When they exchange ideas, each then has two
ideas.

You can't take it with you, and it is pretty hard to keep it while
you're here.

If you can afford the interest,
you probably don't need the loan.

A good gardener has a green thumb—which he sometimes gets
from pulling twenty-dollar bills out of his wallet at the
garden-supply store.

Horse sense is something that horses have to keep them from betting on people.

Statistics show that women spend 85 per cent of the consumer dollar, children 15 per cent, and men the rest.

Some people's budgets are in such a mess, you'd think they were getting advice from the government.

A fool and his money are soon parted. The rest of us wait until income-tax time.

If money is the means to an end, then inflation must be the end to the means.

The fellow who pays cash for his wants soon gets into the habit of not wanting much.

The trouble with today's wage-price spiral is that everybody is trying to climb aboard and nobody wants to get off.

If we had a penny for every word said about pollution, we'd have enough money to eliminate it.

The stork and the obstetrician do have one thing in common—their large bills.

God gives every bird its food,
but he does not throw it into the nest.

An optimist is a man who thinks you can build a $30,000 house for $30,000.

You can't spend yourself rich any more than you can drink yourself sober.

The Internal Revenue Service's take
Must be close to saturation;
Coping with Form 1040
Even taxes the imagination.

Enthusiasm sees only the down payment.

Inflation is what makes chicken feed out of your nest egg.

Money can't buy health, but it can't support sickness either.

With a handful of credit cards, it'd be pretty easy to go for broke—and make it.

Time was when men lost their shirts in the stock markets. Now it's in the supermarkets.

When a habit begins to cost money, it is called a hobby.

If you want to spend your money and have something to show for it, try eating rich food.

If most of us are ashamed of shabby clothes and shoddy furniture, let us be more ashamed of shabby ideas and shoddy philosophies.

One thing we get more of for our money these days is requests.

The politicians' promises of yesterday are the taxes of today.

Inflation is like getting stuck in a traffic jam. You find you are part of the problem, but you can't figure out what to do about it.

Life and taxes are similar in that you finish with both at the same time.

Our forefathers made one mistake. What they should have fought for was representation without taxation.

It would be nice to have taxation without misrepresentation.

If taxes continue to soar, you're going to have to work like a dog to live like one.

Income Tax Advice—Pay It

Poverty is catching—
you can catch it from the Internal Revenue.

The basic test of freedom is perhaps less in what we are free to do than in what we are free not to do.

Diplomacy is the art of letting someone else have your way.

The sign of bureaucracy is when the first person who answers the phone can't help you.

Politics: the art of looking for trouble, finding it everywhere, diagnosing it incorrectly, and applying the wrong remedies.

If a nation values anything more than freedom, it will lose its freedom; and the irony of it is that if it is comfort or money that it values more, it will lose that, too.

Pity the man who believes in communism—he believes in something that doesn't believe in him.

A successful politician is one who can get in the public eye without irritating it.

Laws should be like clothes. They should be made to fit the people they are meant to serve.

The only thing harder to clean up
than a small boy is politics.

Government spending gives you an idea
why laws are called bills.

The preacher prays for all
The lawyer pleads for all
The doctor prescribes for all
The plain citizen pays for all.

The main discomfort of being a middle-of-the-roader is that you get sideswiped by partisans going in both directions.

A sure way to keep crime from paying
is to let the government run it.

Polls are voting places where you stand in line for a chance to decide who will spend your money.

Crime will not decrease until becoming a criminal becomes more dangerous than being a victim.

Everybody wants to eat at the government's table, but nobody wants to do the dishes.

You cannot help men permanently by doing for them what they could and should do for themselves.

Welfare is a program where the donors give steak and potatoes and the recipients get pork and beans.

It may be true that the weak will always be driven to the wall, but it is the task of a just society to see that the wall is climbable.

A politician is a man who approaches every subject
with an open mouth.

The nation which forgets its defenders
will itself be forgotten.

There are two kinds of voters: those who support your candidate and a lot of ignorant, prejudiced fools.

Why do they call them candidates
when so many are far from candid?

There are some politicians who shake your hand before an election and your confidence after.

Recession—when a man next door loses his job.
Depression—when you lose your job.
Panic—when your wife loses her job.

No people is fully civilized where a distinction is drawn between stealing an office and stealing a purse.

A different world cannot be built by indifferent people.

All of our superhighways fall into one of two classes: overcrowded or under construction.

The best way to inspire courteous treatment by other motorists is to drive a police car.

It may be possible to by-pass all of America when the federal highway system is completed.

Give a man a fish, and you feed him for a day. Teach a man to fish and you feed him for life.

The trouble with political jokes
is that sometimes they are elected.

The trouble with socialism is that when people lean on one another, they soon get too weak to stand alone.

It's getting harder and harder to support the government in the style to which it has been accustomed.

In a democracy, the individual enjoys not only the ultimate power, but carries the ultimate responsibility.

Columbus was responsible for the thinking of modern government. He didn't know where he was going when he started; he didn't know where he was when he got there; and he did it on borrowed money.

The major difficulty in cutting down government expenses is that the expenses have votes.

There are many complaints about the weather, but not so many as there would be if the government regulated it instead of predicted it.

Love · Friends · Family · Women

Hating people is like burning down
your own house to get rid of the rats.

The love in your heart wasn't put there to stay. Love isn't love
till you give it away.

Love for the same thing never makes allies. It's always hate for
the same thing.

Service is love in work clothes.

The great and the little have need of one another.

Love is like a mushroom. You never know whether it's the real
thing until it's too late.

Love makes it possible to believe the impossible.

How it improves people for us when we begin to love them.

Love may be blind, but hate is far more so.

Where love rules, there is no will to power.

We sometimes never know love until it is lost.

Isn't it amazing the way nature can produce a beautiful diamond merely by taking a man and putting him under terrific pressure?

Friendship doubles your joys and divides your grief.

Friendships are fragile things, and require as much care in handling as any other fragile and precious things.

Friendship, like a young tree, must be planted in rich soil, watered properly with common sense to establish deep roots, and then grown in the sunshine of time.

Love looks forward, hate looks back,
anxiety has eyes all over the head.

Marriage is an institution held together by three books—
good, cook, and check.

Courage is like love—it must have hope to nourish it.

Respect is love in plain clothes.

Marriage is not a destination—it is a journey.

By the time he whispers, "We were made for each other," she
is already planning alterations.

The love of liberty is the love of others; the love of power is the
love of ourselves.

The only way to have friends is to be one.

If you love life, life will love you back.

Things will improve when the power of love
replaces the love of power.

The hand that gives gathers.

Often, when she says, "No,"
they both live happily ever after, too.

Making marriage work is like running a farm. You have to start
all over again each morning.

The great secret of successful marriage is to treat all disasters as
incidents and none of the incidents as disasters.

The happiest couples are those
who spell "us" with a capital "you."

An optimist is a guy who marries his secretary and expects to
continue dictating.

The trouble in marriage often starts when the man is so busy earning his salt that he forgets his sugar.

You never realize how much a person's voice can change until your wife stops yelling at you and answers the phone.

When Adam was lonely, God created for him not ten friends, but one wife.

Every man needs a wife. Many things go wrong that can't be blamed on the government.

Show me a happily married couple and I'll show you two people unworried about who is the better half.

Any man who thinks he's more intelligent than his wife is married to a smart woman.

Some wives have terrible memories;
they never forget anything.

The goal in marriage is not to think alike, but to think together.

Some like it cold, some like it hot.
Some freeze while others smother.
And by some fiendish, fatal plot,
They marry one another.

He who gives in when he is wrong is wise, he who gives in when he is right is married.

In a marriage, the man is the provider
and the woman the decider.

Don't judge your wife too harshly for her weaknesses. If she didn't have them, chances are she wouldn't have married you.

Today, when newlyweds feather their nests, you'll usually find four parents who have been plucked.

Optimist: a bridegroom who thinks he has no bad habits.

A honeymoon is that short interval between bells and bills.

The biggest drawback to budding love is blooming expense.

Men and women chasing each other
is what makes the human race.

Never be so busy bringing home the bacon
that you forget the applesauce.

One thing all kids save for a rainy day is a lot of energy.

Communication in the home is not improved by loud speakers.

When asked to start a garden,
the first thing many men dig up is an excuse.

You hear about "dumb" animals, but did you ever hear of one
that planted grass seed in May so he'll have to push a lawn
mower in July?

Parents are people who bear infants,
bore teenagers, and board newlyweds.

One sign that summer is almost over: when the air-conditioner
repairman returns your call.

People who sleep like a baby probably don't have one.

A boy is noise with dirt on it.

Home is the place in which we are treated
the best and grumble the most.

Adolescence is the period of rapid changes. Between the ages
of 12 and 17, for example, a parent ages as much as 50 years.

He who believes that where there is smoke there is fire, never
tried cooking on a camping trip.

The most important thing a father can do for his children
is love their mother.

It is hard for parents to lead a child in the straight and narrow
way when they're on the other route.

It is indeed a desirable thing to be well descended, but the
glory belongs to our ancestors.

The man who boasts only of his ancestors confesses that he
belongs to a family that is better dead than alive.

One of the secrets of raising a child properly is knowing when
to give them a hand and where.

It is an unfortunate fact that the youngsters at summer camp
who are the most homesick are those who have dogs at home.

The philosopher who said, "A work well done never needs
doing over," evidently never pulled weeds in the garden or
cleaned a house.

The problems of the world have become so complex that even
the teenagers don't have all the answers.

In the modern household the children are about the only
things left that still have to be washed by hand.

It's when you're safe at home that you wish you were having
an adventure. When you're having an adventure you wish you
were safe at home.

What retirement means to the lady of the house is twice as
much husband on half as much income.

Home is where you can put up your feet
and let down your hair.

Many parents are so anxious to give their children what they
didn't have that they neglect to give them what they did have.

Bringing up children is simple if you don't have any.

Remember the good old days when the only jams kids got into were plum, grape, and blackberry.

It's nice for children to have pets
until the pets start having children.

A MOTHER'S PRAYER:
    Give me patience when little hands
    Tug at me with ceaseless small demands.
    Give me gentle words and smiling eyes,
    And keep my lips from hasty, sharp replies.
    Let me not in weariness, confusion or noise
    Obscure my vision from life's fleeting joys
    That when in years to come my house is still
    Beautiful memories its rooms may fill.

The real problem of your leisure
is to keep other people from using it.

As troublemakers, few outlaws can beat the in-laws.

Nothing makes it easier to resist temptation than a proper bringing-up, a sound set of values—and witnesses.

Children are not things to be molded,
but are people to be unfolded.

Summer is when kids slam the doors they left open all winter.

Parenthood is a gamble. You never know how far you're going to be driven out of your mind.

It is much easier to become a father than to become a man.

If you see handwriting on the wall,
your two-year-old probably found a pencil.

Mealtime is the period when kids sit down to continue eating.

The world's population explosion is everybody's baby.

The perfect hostess opens her heart with her door.

The factory that produces the most
important product is the home.

The greatest influence on a child
begins with the birth of his parents.

A family tree is worth bragging about if it has produced good
timber and not just a lot of nuts.

Any woman who wants a little time to herself
has only to begin washing the dishes.

A man admires a woman not for what she says
but for what she listens to.

Nature gave woman too much power;
the law gives them too little.

If you don't think girls are dynamite, try dropping one.

The better a woman looks, the longer a man does.

Some men permit women to make fools of them;
others are the do-it-yourself type.

A woman is perturbed by what a man forgets—
a man by what a woman remembers.

I don't know of anything better than a woman if you want to
spend money where it will show.

No matter how orderly a woman is by nature, it is a mistake for
her to always be putting her husband in his place.

Never argue with a woman when she's tired—or rested.

A vision at dinner is often a sight at breakfast.

Man once subscribed to the theory of male superiority—then woman canceled his subscription.

Salesmanship is the ability to convince your wife that she would look fat in a fur coat.

it often happens that the apple of a parent's eye is the kid who is rotten to the core.

The average man has probably thought twice about running away from home—once as a child and once as a husband.

If a third of the nation is ill-fed, ill-housed, and ill-clothed—the camping season must be here again.

A good woman is like a good book—entertaining, inspiring and instructive; sometimes a bit too wordy, but when properly bound and decorated, irresistible.

A woman has a better chance of snaring a man
if she keeps her trap shut.

Girls have an unfair advantage over men; if they can't get what they want by being smart, they can get it by being dumb.

Doing a woman's work is like walking down a railroad track; the end seems in sight but never is.

Nothing annoys a housewife so much as having her friends drop in and find her house looking as it usually does.

Ask a woman how she stubbed her toe and she'll say she walked into a chair; ask a man, and he'll say someone left a chair in the middle of the room.

Some women aren't very good at counting calories and they have the figures to prove it.

She's a light eater—as soon as it is light,
she starts eating.

A Time For Learning

Education • Wisdom • Intelligence

If you would make the road to accomplishment a little shorter, go to school a little longer.

Little kids graduate from skipping rope to skipping classes in a very few years.

The trouble with dropouts is not that they cannot see the handwriting on the wall, but that they cannot read it.

To teach is to learn twice.

Kids who say school is a bummer, Often are among the dumber.

The only thing more expensive than education is ignorance.

The end of school brings home to parents what teachers have known for nine months.

Only hungry minds can become educated.

Experience is a good teacher—
and she doesn't allow dropouts.

The gum-chewing student
And cud-chewing cow
Look quite alike
But they're different, somehow.

And what is the difference?
I see it all now—
It's the intelligent look
On the face of the cow.

The direction in which education starts a man
will determine his future life.

Kids used to bring teachers apples;
now they drive them bananas!

Ignorance is not bliss—it is oblivion.

Why do the worst-behaved children in school
always have the best attendance record?

A wise man appears ridiculous in the company of fools.

Most of our inventions have been produced by fairly
uneducated men—maybe they didn't know it couldn't be done.

A thorough education not only pays better wages than hard
labor, but it brings the best of everything else.

People with one track minds
often have derailed trains of thoughts.

You have two chances of making good without working—
slim and none.

Genius has its limitations,
but vanity and stupidity have no limits.

How much you know is not as important
as what you do with what you know.

A closed mind can be awfully stuffy.

An investment in knowledge always pays interest.

Bright people do not cast reflections.

Education pays—unless, of course, you're the educator.

A good idea can never drop into a closed mind.

Television is not only replacing radio—
it's doing a pretty good job on homework too.

Experience is the best teacher,
but the fees are usually high.

Hooky is when a small boy lets his mind wander—
and then follows it.

Education is man going from cocksure ignorance
to thoughtful uncertainty.

Said the dean to his college professors,
"Be kind to the kids who get A's—
They'll come back to our institution
And succeed you as profs someday."

"And also take care of those students
Whose marks are B's and C's—
They'll send their own children back
   to us
To get their college degrees."

"And what about the others
Who often wind up with D's?
Treat them the best of all because
We'll depend on endowments from these."

A rather important contemporary problem:
too many unintelligent intellectuals.

A handful of common sense is worth an arm-load of learning.

You never lose if you learn from losing.

What wisdom can you find that is greater than kindness?

Most people underestimate their own brain power
and overestimate the other person's.

Knowledge is only potential power.

By the time we recognize a man's brilliance we've forgotten the
stupid questions he asked to get that way.

There is no more terrible sight than ignorance in action.

If you keep your mind sufficiently open,
people will throw a lot of rubbish into it.

Heads seldom swell until the mind stops growing.

In order that all men may be taught the truth, it is necessary
that all likewise should learn to hear it.

There are many shining qualities in the mind of man, but there
is none so useful as discretion . . . without it, learning is
pedantry and wit impertinence.

A little learning is a dangerous thing. Just ask any student who
has brought home a bad report card.

One thorn of experience is worth
a whole wilderness of warning.

Learned men carry their wealth with them.

The object of education is to prepare the young
to educate themselves throughout their lives.

It is hard for an empty sack to stand upright.

Our poor students do not need special education
as much as they need special teaching.

If the cost of education continues to rise, education will
become as expensive as ignorance.

The thinking that guides your intelligence is much more
important than how much intelligence you may have.

Never let your schooling interfere with your education.

Opinions of thinking men change constantly—
like growing children.

When high school kids wear rags today,
We call it self-expression;
When I was young and dressed this way,
We called it the Depression.

The true test of intelligence is not how much we know how to
do, but how we behave when we don't know what to do.

Three stages of a teacher's education:
1: He realizes he doesn't know anything
about the way students act.
2. He thinks he knows all about the way students act.
3. He realizes he was right the first time.

The test of a truly educated man is what he is, and what he
thinks, and what his mind absorbs, or dreams, or creates, when
he is alone.

Reading is to the mind what exercise is to the body.

Don't hesitate to ask dumb questions—
they're easier to handle than dumb mistakes.

Wisdom is knowing when you cannot be wise.

Having a lot on your mind isn't necessarily
a sign of intelligence.

They know enough who know how to learn.

Keep the gold and keep the silver, but give us wisdom.

If you don't know, admit it—then find out.

The wise man hurries less but makes more progress.

Attitudes are often more important than intelligence.

A genius often is one who shoots at something no one else can
see, and hits it.

Knowledge is knowing facts; wisdom is knowing what to do
with the facts you know.

Knowledge is a comfortable and necessary retreat and shelter
for us in an advanced age; and if we do not plant it while
young, it will give us no shade when we grow old.

The question not asked cannot be answered.

A lot of people get through thinking
before they think things through.

Fight truth decay.

The chief aim of wisdom is to enable one to bear
with the stupidity of the ignorant.

Truth will be truth regardless of lack of understanding,
disbelief, or ignorance on the part of anyone.

Ignorance is when you don't know anything
and then somebody finds out.

If you are not a thinking man,
to what purpose are you a man at all?

Some people could be brainwashed with an eyedropper.

There is nobody so irritating as somebody with less intelligence and more sense than we have.

No man is free who is not master of himself.

It is not so important to be serious as it is to be serious about important things. The monkey wears an expression of seriousness which would do credit to any scholar, but the monkey is serious because he itches.

If you burn the candle at both ends,
you may not be as bright as you think.

Everyone pays—either attention or dearly.

One way to learn manners is from those who have none.

The greatest and noblest pleasure which men can have in this world is to discover new truths. And the next is to shake off old prejudices.

Genius is not spontaneous combustion. It is a trail of sparks from a grindstone.

Shallow thinkers seldom make deep impressions.

Wisdom comes only with experience,
and experience comes only with time.

Facts do not cease because they are ignored.

Patience is the companion of wisdom.

Genius is often perseverance in disguise.

Frown—at least you'll get credit for thinking.

a TiMe FoP TaLKiNG

Speaking • Gossip • Difficulties

Once there were things people couldn't talk about,
but now they can't talk about anything else.

The best time to hold your tongue is the time you feel like you
must say something or bust.

People often regret speech—silence, never.

It often shows fine command of language to say nothing.

The only gracious way to accept an insult is to ignore it; if you
can't ignore it, top it; if you can't top it, laugh at it; if you can't
laugh at it, it's probably deserved.

Ever notice how many people are mistaken
at the top of their voice?

If nobody ever said anything unless he knew what he was talking about, a ghostly hush would descend upon the earth.

If you do not understand my silence, you will not understand my words.

The hardest thing for some people to say in 25 words or less is "Good-bye."

Few people have convictions—the majority have opinions.

Too often when you tell a secret it goes in one ear and in another.

A moving mouth does not require a working brain.

Talk not of yourself; others will do that for you.

Putting your best foot forward at least keeps it out of your mouth.

Blessed are the brief, for they shall have lower phone bills.

Laryngitis offers one compensation—people will believe anything that is whispered.

If you are a man of few words, you won't have to take so many of them back.

You don't have to be in a car to run people down.

Some people speak twice before they think.

Who thinks an inch, but talks a yard, needs a kick of the foot.

Never trust a woman who tells her real age. A woman like that would tell anything.

Blessed are those who have nothing to say, and who cannot be persuaded to say it.

Some people would rather be wrong than silent.

The secret to being tiresome is to tell everything you know.

Laziness is often a motive for unnecessary talking.

To get the best of an argument, keep out of it.

People will listen a great deal more patiently when you explain your mistakes than when you explain your successes.

If it had been intended for man to talk twice as much as listen, he would have been given two mouths and one ear.

Many who have the gift of gab do not know how to wrap it up.

The best way to get the last word is to apologize.

After all has been said and done, you usually find that more has been said than done.

Most loudmouths have an echo chamber between their ears.

Some people claim they hate to talk about themselves, but seldom enough to refrain.

If you don't believe in carefully choosing your words, think of the difference between "You look like the breath of spring" and "You look like the end of a hard winter."

When your heart is afire,
some sparks will fly out of your mouth.

Learning to speak in two or more languages is not nearly as hard as learning to keep your mouth shut in one.

Some folks say the squeaking wheel gets the grease, but others point out that it is the first one to be replaced.

Good communication is as stimulating as black coffee—
and just as hard to sleep after.

A word to the wise is usually unnecessary.

A loose tongue often leads to loose teeth.

Remember when the unmentionables were also unseeables?

Pleasant words are as honeycomb, sweet to the soul, and health to the bones.

Some speakers drive facts home; others, the audience.

Pity the woman with some hot gossip, and a dead phone.

The only person who listens to both sides of a family argument is the person next door.

Some people have gear trouble.
They talk in high gear and think in low gear.

The older I get, the more I listen
to people who don't talk much.

The cruelest lies are often told in silence.

You will never hear anyone accuse you of having a biased opinion as long as his agrees with yours.

Biting remarks are often the result of snap judgements.

Words, like eyeglasses, blur everything
that they do not make more clear.

Words, like tranquil waters behind a dam, can become reckless and uncontrollable torrents of destruction when released without caution and wisdom.

Funny thing about corn—in the Midwest it's measured by the foot, in the South by the fifth, and on television by the hour.

You cannot go around giving people a piece of your mind without making them think you are not all there.

Big words don't always convey big thoughts.

We would have no objection to people who eat like sparrows if they would only stop that everlasting chirping about it.

After-dinner speeches need a lot of shortening, too.

Cutting remarks sever friendships.

It is useless to try to hold a person to anything he says while he's madly in love, drunk, or running for office.

Whatever your grade or position, if you know how and when to speak, and when to remain silent, your chances of real success are proportionately increased.

When a speech is boiled down, it isn't so dry.

Subtlety is the art of saying what you think and getting out of range before it is understood.

The fellow who brags about how smart he is,
wouldn't if he were.

Criticism is like fertilizer—the right amount does wonders, but too much is fatal.

If anyone speaks evil of you, let your life be so
that none will believe him.

The dimmer the light, the more scandal power it has.

Tact is the ability to make a person see the lightning without letting him feel the bolt.

Tact is a person's ability to describe others as they see themselves.

The most pointed remarks are not always the sharpest.

Dull wits lead to sharp tongues.

Blunt people can get to the point very quickly.

Never say all that you know, but always know all that you say.

It is just as easy to give good advice to yourself as to others—and quite as useless.

Free advice is usually worth the price.

He who knows little soon repeats it.

It's amazing how many things people turn on and off during the day—including people.

Usually the first screw that gets loose in the head is the one that controls the tongue.

A person who talks a lot will occasionally say something wise—but chances are no one will be listening.

Who can refute a sneer?

A yawn is a silent shout.

Advice is like mushrooms;
consuming the wrong kind might prove fatal.

To save face, keep part of it shut.

The people sensible enough to give good advice are usually sensible enough to give none.

Each person filters incoming messages through the prism of his prejudices.

A flatterer is one who says things to your face that he wouldn't say behind your back.

A word, a look, an accent, may affect the destiny not only of individuals, but of nations. He is a bold man who calls anything a trifle.

When you give honest advice, have one foot out the door.

The secret of the man who is universally interesting is that he is universally interested.

Beware of the man who says he has an open mind.
He often has a mouth to match it.

Always be sure your brain is in gear
before you put your mouth in motion.

Every time you open your mouth,
you let people look into your life.

If you ask enough people, you can usually find somebody
who'll advise you to do what you were going to do anyway.

Remember not only to say the right thing in the right place, but far more difficult still, to leave unsaid the wrong thing at the tempting moment.

If we could see ourselves as others see us,
we'd never speak to them again.

There may not be much to see in a small town,
but what you hear makes up for it.

The only person who makes a success in running other people down is the elevator boy.

Why can we remember the tiniest details that have happened to us, and not remember how many times we have told it to the same person?

You can't dig up much dirt
without getting yourself in a hole.

Letting things go in one ear and out the other is bad enough, but it's worse when things go in one ear, get all mixed up, and come out the mouth.

Just because a rumor is idle
doesn't mean that it isn't working.

A sharp tongue is the only edged tool
that grows keener with constant use.

Why must the phrase "It is none of my business" always be
followed by the word "but"?

Knowing what is none of your business
is just as important as doing what is.

Plastic surgery can do anything with a human nose except keep
it out of other people's business.

Nothing improves a person's hearing more than praise.

Hot heads and cold hearts never solved anything.

Anyone who keeps a chip on his shoulder can't chop much
wood.

Self-discipline is the main factor in building character.

Despondence is the most unprofitable feeling
a man can indulge in.

Truth needs no crutches. If it limps, it's a lie.

Pollution is one of the things everybody talks about and
everybody does something about—like contributes to it.

To err is human, but it takes a better excuse the next time.

A dentist is the only man who prefers the company of a man
with a hole in his head.

Misery loves company, but company doesn't love misery.

The trouble with today's individualists is that they are getting
too hard to tell apart.

No one can make you feel inferior without your permission.

People who fly into a rage always make a bad landing.

Jealousy makes us smaller in the hearts of our friends, weaker in the eyes of our adversaries, and defenseless in the hands of our enemies.

We can destroy ourselves by cynicism and disillusion, just as effectively as by bombs.

Standing on your dignity makes for poor footing.

The amount of pain we inflict upon others is directly proportional to the amount we feel within ourselves.

Maturity begins when we're content to feel we're right about something without the necessity to prove someone else wrong.

We are inclined to react most violently to our own faults when we see them demonstrated by other people.

Criticism, like rain, should be gentle enough to nourish a man's growth without destroying his roots.

Flattery is great if you don't inhale.

There are more self-marred people in the world than there are self-made.

You can't shake hands with a clenched fist.

You never get a second chance to make a good first impression.

There is no reward for finding fault.

The best way to convince a fool that he is wrong is to let him have his own way.

Maturity is the ability to live with imperfections.

When you dig another out of trouble,
you've a place to bury your own.

Doing an injury puts you below your enemy; revenging one
makes you even with him; forgetting it sets you above him.

If pleasures are greatest in anticipation, just remember that this
is also true of trouble.

To err is human, to forgive takes restraint; to forget you forgave
is the mark of a saint.

A fight starts only with the second blow.

A group of hotheaded men are like a book of matches. It takes
but one to set off the whole group—and destroy itself, too.

There's one thing to be said for inviting trouble—it generally
accepts.

The longer we dwell on our misfortunes,
the greater is their power to harm us.

Push-buttons have taken the place of all kinds of cranks
except human ones.

The most disappointed people in the world
are those who got what's coming to them.

Sin is not only doing something wrong,
but failing to do what is right.

When I hide my emotions, my stomach keeps score.

Not wearing seat belts is a killer of an idea.

Worry has been defined as mental handwringing.

No man ever becomes either very good or very bad suddenly.

The best cure for a small problem is a bigger one.

Why is anyone surprised that cities have problems? It has been our experience that problems tend to go where the people are.

People carried away by their own importance
seldom have far to walk back.

Trouble seems to be one commodity
of which there is no shortage.

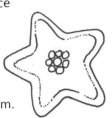

Problems always appear big
when incompetent men are working on them.

The only way to stop smoking
is to just stop—no ifs, ands, or butts.

A man must be big enough to admit his mistakes, smart enough to profit by them, and strong enough to correct them.

The man who doesn't make any mistakes
probably doesn't do much.

Drivers who weave in traffic often wind up in stitches.

A diplomat is anyone who thinks twice before saying nothing.

We all boil at different degrees.

I will never allow anyone to do me
the injury of making me hate him.

Two of the best known finishes for automobiles
are lacquer and liquor.

The best advice is only as good as the use you make of it.

Don't worry about your hair falling out. Just think how it would be if your hair ached and had to be pulled out.

Seat belts are not as confining as wheelchairs.

Seconds count—especially when dieting.

The tragedy of ulcers is that you can have them
and still not be successful.

Many of our suspicions of others
arise from our knowledge of ourselves.

Your character cannot be essentially injured
except by your own acts.

Sometimes it takes a lot of scratching around to get out of a
situation you were just itching to get into.

If a small thing has the power to make you angry, does that not
indicate something about your size?

I have as much patience as the rest of you,
but I don't have time to practice it.

In the presence of trouble some people buy crutches;
others grow wings.

A gossip is a person who talks to you about others. A bore is
one who talks to you about himself. A brilliant
conversationalist is one who talks to you about yourself.

The mouth is the grocer's friend, the dentist's fortune, the
orator's pride, and the fool's trap.

The truth may be as clear as a bell,
but it's not always tolled.

When all is said and done, the only person
easy to deceive is yourself.

A Time For Living

Life • Age • Time

Life is like a taxi—the meter keeps running whether you are getting somewhere or just standing still.

Life is a one-way street. No matter how many detours you take, none of them leads back.

Life is either a daring adventure or nothing.

Cross your bridges before you come to them
and you have to pay the toll twice.

A man's life is 20 years of having his mother ask him where he's going, 40 years of having his wife ask the same question; and at the end, the mourners are wondering, too!

The Garden of Life:
   First plant five rows of P's—
      Presence
      Promptness
      Preparation
      Perserverance
      Purity
   Next, plant three rows of Squash—
      Squash gossip
      Squash indifference
      Squash unjust criticism
   Then plant five rows of Lettuce—
      Let us be faithful to duty
      Let us be unselfish and loyal
      Let us obey the rules and regulations
      Let us be true to our obligations
      Let us love one another
   No garden is complete without Turnips—
      Turn up for meetings
      Turn up with a smile
      Turn up with new ideas
      Turn up with determination to make everything count
for something good and worthwhile.

Life's evening will take on its character
from the day that preceded it.

Are you going places, or just being taken?

Life is about 10% how you make it, and 90% how you take it.

How strange to use "You only live once"
as an excuse to throw it away.

To those who search, life reveals its mystery.

Our days are like suitcases—all the same size; but some persons
seem to be able to pack more into them than others.

Life is not a loose-leaf book.

This is the beginning of a new day. I can waste it or use it for good. What I do today is important because I am exchanging a day of my life for it. When tomorrow comes, the day will be gone forever—leaving in its place something I have traded for it. I want it to be a gain not a loss; good, not evil; success, not failure, in order that I may not regret the price I paid for today.

It is not death that man should fear, but he should fear never beginning to live.

Self-confidence is being overweight, over 50, and wearing shorts while mowing the lawn.

When everything is coming your way,
you're probably in the wrong lane.

That which is beautiful is not always good, but that which is good is always beautiful.

The best reformers the world has ever seen
are those who commence on themselves.

To have lost your reputation is to be dead among the living.

Gardening: a matter of your enthusiasm holding up
until your back gets used to it.

Some people are carbon copies—
others make their own impressions.

Gardening, like all the important and most of the delightful things of life, is worthwhile only when you do it yourself.

The garden is the ONE place
where you don't always reap what you sow.

One of the healthiest ways to gamble is with a spade and a package of garden seeds.

God must have loved plain people—he made so many of them.

Don't be ashamed of your past—write a best-seller.

There is more to life than increasing its speed.

Pluck takes us into a difficulty; nerve brings us out of it.

The next time you're feeling low
And decide that you're a slob
Dig up the last letter you wrote about yourself
When you were out of a job.

Using today to mop up yesterday wipes out tomorrow.

When the days get shorter, the weeks seem to get longer.

Growth is the only evidence of life.

The morning after is when getting up gets you down.

Those who get the greatest kick out of life
are those who kick the least.

The simple—but difficult—key to contentment is to realize that
life in its entirety is a gift, not a right.

We need more wildlife in the wide open
and less in the big cities.

People can be divided into three groups: those who make
things happen, those who watch things happen, and those
who wonder what happened.

Any town is a delightful place
if you are a delightful person.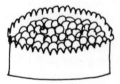

Inconsistency with ourselves
is the great weakness of human nature.

The only people to get even with are those who helped you.

Life is a lot like a grindstone in that it grinds some people down and polishes others up.

In life the things you reach soonest are the bridges you were not going to cross until you came to them.

The ladder of life is full of splinters, but they always prick the hardest when we're sliding down.

Whether life grinds a man down or polishes him up depends on what he is made of.

Up, sluggard, and waste not life,
in the grave will be sleeping enough.

Man's liberty ends when that liberty
becomes the curse of his neighbors.

A man without self-restraint is like a barrel without hoops, and tumbles to pieces.

Courage is the power to let go of the familiar.

Character is what you are in the dark.

You are not mature until you expect the unexpected.

Patience is bitter, but its fruits are sweet.

Poise is looking like an owl after behaving like a jackass.

People become bored, not so much by living, as by not living.

All men command patience,
although few are willing to practice it.

He surely is most in need of another's patience,
who has none of his own.

People who live to do good
seldom complain of their role in life.

Circumstances form the character;
but like petrifying waters, they harden while they form.

Many of life's most valuable things cannot be seen,
weighed, measured, bought, or sold.

Courage is the knowledge of how to fear what ought to be
feared, and how not to fear what ought not to be feared.

Every minute a person spends worrying about dying is just one
minute that a fellow might as well be dead.

If you come to the end of a perfect day,
check back very carefully.

Consider how hard it is to change yourself and you'll
understand what little chance you have of trying to change
others.

Men show their character in nothing more clearly than by what
they think laughable.

Imagination was given to man to compensate him for what he
is not, and a sense of humor was provided to console him for
what he is.

The oldest, shortest words—"yes" and "no"—are those which
require the most thought.

Men and rivers get crooked
by following the line of least resistance.

This would be a fine world if all men showed as much patience
all the time as they do while they're waiting for a fish to bite.

A great deal of what we see
depends on what we are looking for.

An autobiography usually reveals nothing bad about its writer
except his memory.

In small towns, alcoholics are never anonymous.

All sunshine makes a desert.

If you can't stand solitude, maybe you bore others, too.

The longest journey is the journey inward.

Conceit is God's gift to little men.

Each day's sunset gives one less day to life,
but one more day to remember.

Character is the tree; reputation is the shadow.

Yesterday is experience—tomorrow is hope—today is getting
from one to the other as best we can.

The test of good manners is being able to
put up pleasantly with bad ones.

Seeing ourselves as others see us wouldn't do much good,
because most of us wouldn't believe what we saw.

Drive carefully: watch the car in back
of the one in front of you.

The trick is to hold opinions
without letting opinions hold you.

Life is like a piano. What you get out of it
depends on how you play it.

It's important for people to know what you stand for. It's
equally important that they know what you won't stand for.

The rule for traveling abroad is to take our common sense with
us, and leave our prejudices behind.

The deepest principle in human nature
is the craving to be appreciated.

The claim of equality is made only by those who feel themselves to be in some way inferior.

Prejudice is pollution of the mind.

Behavior is a mirror in which everyone shows his image.

It takes both rain and sunshine to make a rainbow.

If you treat people right they will treat you right—
90 per cent of the time.

Nothing makes them the good old days so much
as a good old imagination.

Anyone who ever tried to swat flies with a television set will
appreciate the daily newspaper all the more.

Character is made by what you stand for;
reputation by what you fall for.

Friendship is like money—it is easier made than kept.

Fog is stuff it's dangerous to drive in—
especially if it is mental.

He who stands for nothing will fall for anything.

Humor is a hole that lets the sawdust out of a stuffed shirt.

Don't drive as if you own the road;
drive as if you own the car.

Any man can stand up to his opponents; give me the man who
can stand up to his friends.

Dreams are the magic threads, intricately woven into life, that
give us reason for being.

Tomorrow is simply an extension of today, and likely won't be
any better or worse than today—unless we make it so.

Those who live it up may also have to live it down.

Everybody has to be somebody to somebody to be anybody.

Chewing gum may be hazardous to
the mental health of those about you.

You show courtesy to others not because they are gentlemen,
but because you are one.

Tact is the ability to stay in the middle
without getting caught there.

Time wounds all heels.

Our opinion of people depends less upon what we see in them
than in what they make us see in ourselves.

Let there be peace on earth and let it begin with me.

Flattery is warming yourself by an artificial fireplace.

Too often we seek justice for just us.

A man can stand a lot as long as he can stand himself.

Do you realize that one in every four Americans is unbalanced?
Think of your three closest friends. If they seem okay, then
you're the one.

Rhyme for pedestrian safety:
    Bill looked
    Joe didn't
    Bill is
    Joe isn't.

Life has a way of overcharging a fellow for overindulgence.

Calories don't count—they multiply.

Traffic warning sign: "Heads you win—cocktails you lose."

Even though the automobile replaced the horse, the driver should stay on the wagon.

The automobile did away with the horses. Now, it's working on the rest of us.

Overweight is what happens when you take the butter with the sweet.

The body is the baggage you must carry through life. The more excess baggage, the shorter the trip.

Some rights are worth dying for.
The right of way is not one of them.

Your own soul is nourished when you are kind;
it is destroyed when you are cruel.

There is often less danger in the things we fear than in the things we desire.

We used to blame bad people on the environment. Now we blame the environment on bad people.

Vanity is the result of a delusion
that someone is paying attention.

An optimist is a person who starts working on a crossword puzzle with an ink pen.

Don't you wish some of the things
you don't like anyhow were bad for you?

Not many sounds in life exceed in interest
a knock at the door.

As you travel through life
No matter where you may go,
Keep your eye upon the doughnut
And not upon the hole.

Most of us hate to see a poor loser—or a rich winner.

Eat breakfast like a king, eat lunch like a prince,
but eat dinner like a pauper.

Jogging keeps the spring in your step from becoming rusted.

It is not a tragedy to have only one talent;
the tragedy is in not using it.

Be yourself—who else is better qualified?

Human nature is what we're put in the world to rise above.

Anxiety in human life is what squeaking and grinding are in
machinery that is not oiled. In life, trust is the oil.

Life is like a tennis game; you can't win without serving.

Life's heaviest burden is to have nothing to carry.

Surgeons should be very careful
When they wield the knife.
For underneath their fine incisions
Lurks the culprit—Life!

This minute, too, is part of eternity.

There may not be a cure for every illness,
but there sure is a get-well card.

Some people go through life getting results;
others get consequences.

Everyone wants to get what's coming to him
without getting what he deserves.

Art, like morality, consists in drawing a line somewhere.

It wouldn't be so bad if civilization were only at the crossroads,
but this is one of those cloverleaf jobs.

A man has made at least a start on discovering the meaning of human life when he plants shade trees under which he knows full well he will never sit.

There is nothing certain but the unforeseen.

At age 20 we don't care what the world thinks of us; at 40 we worry about what it is thinking of us; at 60 we discover it wasn't thinking of us at all.

The difference between a man and a boy is the cost of his toys.

One difference between teenagers' faults and ours—
they will probably outgrow theirs.

Denunciation of the young is a necessary part of the hygiene of older people, and greatly assists in the circulation of their blood.

Many people's tombstones should read:
"Died at 40—buried at 70."

It's not how old you are, but how you are old.

When a woman tells you her age, it's all right to look surprised, but don't scowl.

A prune is a plum that has seen better days.

Youth is a time of ferment, not cement.

Youth is glorious, but it isn't a career.

Time deals gently only with those who take it gently.

It takes two kinds of people to make a world—poets to write about the glories of autumn and the rest of us to rake them.

To me, old age is always 15 years older than I am.

Nostalgia is longing for the place you wouldn't move back to.

The seasons slip by and, before you know it, it's time for the bulbs you didn't plant last fall not to come up.

The best thing about spring is that it comes when it is most needed.

A boy gets to be a man when a man is needed.

The only time a woman wishes she were a year older is when she is expecting a baby.

The big shock in becoming middle-aged is that you discover you keep on growing older, even after you are old enough.

Middle age is when the young complain to you about the old and the old complain to you about the young.

Five B's of middle age: baldness, bridgework, bifocals, baywindows and bunions.

Middle age is when you begin to exchange emotions for symptoms.

The error of youth is to believe that intelligence is a substitute for experience, while the error of age is to believe that experience is the substitute for intelligence.

Experts say our country is facing another energy shortage. For once we middle-agers are in tune with the times.

Teenagers ponder, "Who am I?"
As if one needs unmasking.
"You won't find out," I'm apt to sigh,
"Just sitting there asking."

We've put more effort into helping folks reach old age than in helping them enjoy it.

Youth looks ahead. Old age looks back.
Middle age looks worried.

It's not that we're more agreeable
As the keen eyesight of youth passes;
All that nodding up and down
Is adjusting to bifocal glasses.

Getting old is merely a matter of feeling your corns
more than your oats.

Careful grooming may make you look 20 years younger, but it
still won't fool a flight of stairs.

Old age is when your thoughts change from passion to
pension.

By the time a man gets to greener pastures,
he can't climb the fence.

You've reached middle age when all you exercise is caution.

The secret of living to be 100
becomes less attractive as you get older.

Our generation never got a break. When we were young they
taught us to respect our elders, and now that we're older they
tell us to listen to our youth.

The older a person is the noisier the youngsters are.

A fellow who leads a double life
often gets through it in half the time.

America seems to be the only nation on earth that asks its
teenagers what to do about world affairs and tells its
golden-agers to go out and play.

At a certain age some people's minds close up;
they live on intellectual fat.

It's middle age when your clothes no longer fit—
and it's you who need the alteration.

Of all liars, the smoothest and most convincing is memory.

Nothing ages people like not thinking.

You can tell when you hit middle age by the way it hits back.

How could a teenager not be confused. Half the adults tell him to find himself and the other half tell him to get lost.

It is the malady of our age that the young are so busy teaching us that they have no time left to learn.

Just when you make it over the hump,
you find that you are over the hill.

I wish I were what I was when I wanted to be what I am now.

The year is always portrayed as an old man or a baby. Like most people, it never gets any attention when it's middle-aged.

You're getting old when it takes longer
to rest than to get tired.

You must change with the times—unless you are big enough to change the times.

To keep young, associate with young people. To get old in a hurry, try to keep up with them.

Having fun is like buying insurance—
the older you get, the more it costs.

A lot of people feel they reach 40 prematurely.

You have reached middle age
when a night out is followed by a day in.

Another uncomfortable feeling—
maybe the gray hair isn't premature.

The good old days perhaps were, because we were younger.

Happiness · Trust · God

Success is getting what you want;
happiness is wanting what you get.

Someone to love, something to do, and something to look
forward to—these are the ingredients of a happy life.

Trifles make up the happiness or the misery of mortal life.

Happiness is a by-product of an effort
to make someone else happy.

Smiling is contagious—frowning outrageous.

Most of the shadows of this life are caused
by our standing in our own sunshine.

Keep your face to the sunshine and you cannot see the
shadow.

There is no cosmetic for beauty like happiness.

Happiness is a way-station between too little and too much.

Of all the unhappy people in the world, the unhappiest are
those who have not found something they want to do.

Unhappiness is not knowing what we want
and killing ourselves to get it.

We can complain because the rose bushes have thorns or
rejoice because thorn bushes have roses.

No man can be happy unless he feels
his life is in some way important.

It is not easy to find happiness in ourselves, and it is not
possible to find it elsewhere.

Kindness is the golden chain
by which society is bound together.

Anyone who is happy all the time must be mad.

A laugh is worth one hundred groans on any market.

Grief can take care of itself; but to get the full value of joy, you
must have somebody to divide it with.

Real joy comes not from ease or riches or from the praise of
men, but from doing something worthwhile.

Laughter is a tranquilizer with no side effects.

Joys are bubble-like; what makes them bursts them, too.

Kindness is never wasted. If it has no effect on the recipient, at least it benefits the bestower.

When you look at the world in a narrow way, how narrow it seems! When you look at it in a mean way, how mean it is! When you look at it selfishly, how selfish it is! But when you look at it in a broad, generous, friendly spirit, what wonderful people you find in it.

Worry does not empty tomorrow of its trouble.
It does empty today of its strength.

Kindness is a warm breeze in a frigid climate, a radiant heat that melts the icebergs of fear, distrust, unhappiness.

Laughter is the sun that drives winter from the human face.

In about the same degree as you are helpful, you will be happy.

To be without some of the things you want
is an indispensable part of happiness.

The world is like a mirror; frown at it and it frowns at you; smile, and it smiles, too.

There's a clue to our troubled society in *Webster's Unabridged Dictionary*. It devotes sixty-two column-inches to the definition of "take" and only twenty-two column-inches to "give."

Health is the thing that makes you feel
that now is the best time of the year.

We have no more right to consume happiness without producing it than to consume wealth without producing it.

Real happiness is more of a habit than a goal, more of an attitude than an attainment.

We cannot hold a torch to light another's path
without brightening our own.

Those who seek for much are left in want of much. Happy is he
to whom God has given with a sparing hand, as much as is
enough.

It would be a happier world if complaints came only from folks
who have something to complain about.

A smile is the light in the window of your face that tells others
that your heart is at home.

A single sunbeam is enough to drive away many shadows.

Happiness is the companion of cheerfulness,
not the creature of circumstances.

Happiness is what overtakes us when we forget ourselves,
when we learn to open our eyes in optimism and close the
door in the face of defeat.

Be dissatisfied enough to improve,
but satisfied enough to be happy.

All that we send into the lives of others
comes back into our own.

Happiness is a butterfly which, when pursued, is always just
beyond your grasp; but which, if you sit down quietly, may
alight on you.

Though we travel the world over to find the beautiful, we must
carry it with us or we find it not.

Kindness is very indigestible.
It disagrees with very proud stomachs.

When a deep injury is done to us,
we never recover until we forgive.

The flowers of tomorrow are in the seeds of today.

He that does good to another also does good to himself.

One of the most important trips a man can make is that involved in meeting the other fellow half-way.

What a man thinks in his heart, he advertises with his face.

Blessed are those who can give without remembering, and take without forgetting.

Did you give him a life?
He's a brother of man,
And bearing all the burden he can.
Did you give him a smile?
He was downcast and blue:
A smile would have helped him to
   battle it through.

Did you give him a hand?
He was slipping downhill:
And the world, so I fancied,
Was using him ill.
Did you give him a word?
Did you show him the road?
Or did you just let him
Go on with his load?

Solitude is an excellent companion
for those who are at peace with themselves.

Like the bread without the spreadin', like the puddin' without the sauce, like a mattress without beddin', like a cart without a hoss, like a door without a latchstring, like a fence without a stile, like a dry and barren creek bed is a face without a smile.

The greatest pleasure is to do a good action by stealth and have it found out by accident.

We win happiness when we lose ourselves in service to others.

An ounce of apology beats a pound of loneliness.

No man stands as straight as when he stoops to help someone.

Happiness is to be found along the way—not at the end of the road—for then the journey is over.

The kindness planned for tomorrow doesn't count for today.

There is a fine line between helping people
and interfering with their lives.

One of the most difficult things to give away is kindness, for it is usually returned.

Although your smiles go many miles,
You need not lose their track;
So smile away, and every day
You'll meet them coming back.

Fate served me meanly and I laughed at her, and along came Happiness and said: "I came to see what you were laughing at."

Laughter is the shortest distance between people.

You can do very little with faith,
but you can do nothing without it.

Fear God and other fears will disappear.

He gives twice who gives quickly.

The best way to know God is to love many things.

All I have seen teaches me to trust the Creator for all I have not seen.

If the head and the body are to be well, you must begin by curing the soul.

Our great-grandfathers called it the Holy Sabbath; our grandfathers, the Sabbath; our fathers, Sunday; but today we call it the Weekend.

Faith will never die as long as
colored seed catalogues are printed.

A religion that is small enough for our understanding would not be large enough for our needs.

There are two ways of spreading light—to be the candle, or the mirror that reflects it.

Nobody will know what you mean by saying that "God is love" unless you act it as well.

Some families think the Sunday morning church is like a convention. Each sends a delegate.

Wrinkles should only indicate where smiles have been.

If you can laugh at it, you can live with it.

May You Always Have Enough . . .
    happiness to keep you sweet,
    trials to keep you strong,
    sorrows to keep you human,
    hope to keep you happy,
    failure to keep you humble,
    success to make you eager,
    friends to give you comfort,
    wealth to meet your needs,
    enthusiasm to look for tomorrow,
    faith to banish depression,
    determination to make each day
    better than the day before.

If God had believed in permissiveness,
He would have given us the Ten Suggestions.

A merry heart causeth good healing, but a broken spirit drieth up the bones.

God will mend a broken heart
if you will give him all the pieces.

Let me be a little kinder,
Let me be a little blinder
To the faults of those about me;
Let me be when I am weary
Just a little bit more cheery;
Let me serve a little better
Those that I am striving for.
Let me be a little meeker
With the brother who is weaker;
Let me think more of my neighbor
And a little less of me.

If it is true absence makes the heart grow fonder, some people must really love their church.

The hardest math to master is that
which enables us to count our blessings.

Young men want to be faithful and are not; old men want to be faithless and cannot.

It is difficult to make a man miserable while he feels he is worthy of himself and claims kindred to the great God who made him.

If more people abided by the tablets brought down by Moses from Mount Sinai, they'd need fewer tablets from the druggist.

A good sermon is one that goes over
your head on Sunday—and hits a neighbor.

Life without faith is like a car without gas. It will go downhill, but makes very little up-hill progress.

No one worth possessing can be quite possessed.

When the darkest hour is present, it is always near the dawn.

It's easy to have a balanced personality. Just forget your troubles as easily as you do your blessings.

If you can't be thankful for what you receive,
be thankful for what you escape.

Every person is on God's most-wanted list.

Thanksgiving is the recognition of the big gap between what God has done for us and what we have done for God and others.

A daily look in "the Good Book" will make us more lovable and the day more livable.

Please be patient—God isn't finished with you yet.

Money may never get a man into heaven,
but it has put many on the church board.

He who seeks God has already found him.

Doubt isn't the opposite of faith;
it is an element of faith.

It is not the work of life, but the worry of life that robs us of strength and breaks down our faith.

Learn to pause—or nothing worthwhile will catch up with you.

Faith carries the light of truth
which eliminates the shadow of doubt.

Work for the Lord. The pay isn't much, but the retirement is out of this world.

Geology gives us an understanding of the patience of God.

Too many people use religion as a bus—they ride it only when it is going their way.

Only he who reads the Scriptures
discovers how they speak to modern life.

God is always a good God.

If you hold your religion lightly,
you are sure to let it slip.

Without faith, we are as stained-glass windows in the dark.

The love of God is broader than the measure of man's mind.

Anything in life worth having and worth working for
is worth praying for.

Lord, grant me patience, but I want it right now.

If you see someone without a smile, give him one of yours.

If your day is hemmed with prayer,
it is less likely to unravel.

Hope is patience with the lamp lit.

Man's greatest power lies in the power of prayer.

God is the sum of all possibilities.

Nothing ever built arose to touch the skies unless some man dreamed that it should, some man believed that it could, and some man willed that it must.

If you're ever going to love me,
love me now, while I can know
All the sweet and tender feelings
which from real affection flow.
Love me now, while I am living;
do not wait till I am gone
And then chisel it in marble
warm love words on ice-cold
stone.
I won't need your kind caresses
when the grass grows o'er my face;
I won't crave your love or kisses
in my last low resting place.
So, then, if you love me any, if
it's but a little bit,
Let me know it now while living;
I can own and treasure it.

It is not the differences between people that cause problems; it's the indifference.

Experience has proven that defeat can be turned into victory when we have the necessary dedication. The strength to go on struggling and salvaging what can be salvaged has saved many lives from disaster.

The deepest feeling always shows itself in silence.

Alcohol preserves everything except secrets.

Just stand aside and watch yourself go by;
Think of yourself as "he" instead of "I" . . .
Pick flaws; find fault; forget the man is you
And strive to make your estimate ring true.